Sukoon

Sukanya Singh

BookLeaf Publishing

India | USA | UK

Presentation by *BookLeaf Publishing*

Web: www.bookleafpub.com

E-mail: info@bookleafpub.com

ISBN: 9789363312869

First edition 2024

DEDICATION

Hi everyone,

The intention of writing a book has come into my life with the many ups and downs and many circumstances where I do not find anyone to share my emotions and thoughts. I started writing.

I give gratitude to my spiritual connection which comes from my Mother and my strong nature which comes from my father, which has led me to experience everything with love, honesty and bravery and also give me a deep connection with spiritual life.

Everything has given me much more to write and to experience the poetry world.

ACKNOWLEDGEMENT

I would acknowledge the extraordinary effort of BookLeaf Publishing, which has given me the opportunity to write and show our untold emotions in the form of words and books.

This opportunity is a golden door that has opened for me to bring my feelings and emotions in the form of a book.

The vision of writing has only come from the real events of life and also from the people who stand by my side like the letter "A" in the alphabet.

Standing always first and showing me the path of all the next alphabets.

PREFACE

I have been writing and formatting poems since my childhood, as my life has given me many opportunities to embrace the raw journey of life.

We all come from one source and return to the same; travel time gives us the opportunity to experience every event in a different way. Every poem mentioned in this book is experienced and written with real emotions.

What I lived, and what I experienced is what I have written in this book.

The "Sukoon" of life is everything, what is written with emotions.

Trust, visualize and read with your complete awareness to understand the life event, that is more beautiful and less admired by us.

The Sunset

Sky is painted the color bright,
A sunset's end with wondrous light

Mountain's silhouette so grand
As day has given command to night.

As all the twinkling stars are ready to shine.
The stars twinkle, like diamonds bright.

What a celestial show with mountain's beauty
and delight
As night falls again, Sun takes the flight.

The Forest

Stretching high and touching the sky
Every tree in the forest is talking to me,

As I walk on the green and soft floor,
I breathe in deep, the scent of pine.

I surrender my everything to this beautiful
design,
The forest is a wonderful place,
Where nature's beauty does embrace
and its heart holds the grace

That brings me peace and a sense of space,
Let me walk a little more
To explore its secret evermore.

The Moon on the Mountain

The moon on the mountain illuminates so bright,
Cold breeze is touching the mountain's high

Stars are twinkling like diamonds bright
Sound of river is keeping everything alive,

Depth of the dark valley is only witnessed by the
moon's light
What a scenic view, the Moon is kissing the
mountain's head in the silent night.

Where the night is still and the world is at its
peace.

The Mother Earth

I know, we belong to you
You always nurture us and let us grow

Your unconditional love given us the courage
To make roads, buildings and many more.

Oh Mother Earth,
You whisper the secret of ancient lore,
Where trees tell their life before.

All great and small creatures are yours.
Your love for all is always pure.

You are a wonderful gift for us, forever new.

Tales of a River

Dear Human,

I am the source of life, and a treasure true.
I am worth more than a gem, who nourishes and
cleanses the land.

I flow smooth and free, my water simmers in the
sun's glee.
My banks are lined with trees that are so tall,
Do not cut them at all,

My depth is the home to the fish in space,
Let them breathe and stay.

I take the round to all the ground, I nurture every
one of you.
Do not make me dirty Human,
As, I am the big blessing and a scary roar.

I shape the land, with a steady hand.
I can give and I can take though,
Your love for me will decide soon,

Whether, I continue my journey with grace
Or, I leave the land with NO TRACE.

What do we know?

What do we know, of the world beyond the sky!
Is it a place of wonder and might?
A place where only imagination can fly,
A place that exists in the form of divine

Beyond the time zone and with natural truth,
It is just a place or a completely different space,
Where everything is in leisure.

What do we know of the world below the ocean
deep and wide?
Where many creatures are at play.
Where stones illuminate with the water and
grass changes the colours.
No one can dive deep, as the secret of oceans is
bay.

Beyond the Mountain

I saw the world beyond the mountain,
A world of wonder, untouched and serene,

A land of tranquil
A land of light, full of valleys with clean sky.

Where mountain's peak reaching to the sky deep,
Where rivers flow and waters play,
And life abounds in every way.

In the world beyond the mountain,
The sun shines bright and the moon glows with grace.
A Gentle breeze stirs the leaves,
And Trees stand tall with peace,

Let us venture,
Let us explore,
The world beyond the mountain's door.

Darkest Night

Some light in the darkest night,
Has given me a hope of life

I lost all my good divine and,
Uncertainty has shown the path of hopelessness
Where my soul shivers while spending alone
time,

I want to shred off everything to release my
burden of life,
And, I was waiting for the perfect time.

But, this light in the darkest night
Has given me hope for life.

Gratitude!

The Rain

I am getting the earthy scent,
So fresh and new
Fills the air and invigorates me

As I stand in the rain, and let it soak me whole
My worries wash away
My heart becomes unspoken

The rain continues and soaks the ground
And brings the new life all around,

The soil becomes a sight to see
A boggy mess, dark and glee
Leaves are shining on the tree
As Rain has left its trace.

Heatwave

The heat index soars, it is hard to bear
A heatwave's wrath, we cannot share

The sky is hazy, The air is still
As we sweat and swelter
Our will is ill.

The world outside, a furnace - like hell,
Many creatures are dying, because of you
heatwave

You are burning our forest
Our mountains are standing with ashes.
We are suffering under your fiery reign,
Our thirst for coolness in the vein

We are dreaming of a cooling shower
And hoping that, you will soon cower.

Nothingness

Nothing can be claimed in this world
Nothing can be hold

Nothing can be proven
Nothing can be pulled apart
Nothing can be taken for granted
Nothing can be done with hate

Nothing can be handled
Nothing can be lose

Life is a flow of river
Where we can only go with the flow
And snooze some moment
To live a little more.

If we Would

If we would go back the days, our parents got
married
We would love them as a guardian
And give them a choice to see the world with
new eyes.

We would hug them everyday to show that love
needs no boundaries,
And taught them to live life the way they want
to,

We would explain to them, that societies are
only here to say
You be strong, choose your path and free
yourself,
We would laugh everyday with them,
We would dance on every beat of the life's event,
And make them understand
That happiness is more important than the rituals
and norms of astrology.

Unknown

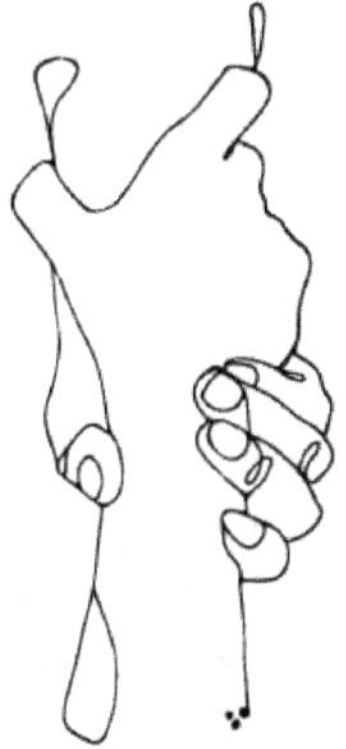

I met the unknown, on the toughest road
My hand was shivering, as I was heading
towards the miserable zone.

I could have lost completely, before he came and
hold
That night,
The stormy wind was so high
That washes all my pain, and kept silent all my
vein

I was not seeking anyone at that time,
But he came as a counterpart of divine,
His endless talks were making me somehow
fine.

We have shared many secrets and
Also, I maintained the silence many times.

What an astonishing bond formed, that would
never fade,
Through any trails and storms, it would stand
tall.

A silent promise, that would never fall,
Far in the silence, a love was born
A love that would last, until dawn.

SHE

Her strength is like a mountain,
And, grace is like a flower
She dances with the wind
And, sings in the shower
She laughs like a joyful sound
And love like a canvas.

She embraces every journey with love and
elegance
She has uncountable pain though,
She cries many times like rain
She screams in showers too
She holds herself tight in emotional storms

She fights everyday a battle with the world and
herself too,
But through it all,
She stands like a tower strong,

With an unharmed spirit and a flame of hope
Where she can weave her dream again.

City Of Love

Where the streets are paved with gold and hearts
are divine
People are singing in love, and with joy in their
eyes

It is a city of love,
Where parks are in bloom with flowers
And roads are colourful and delight

Here river flows gently with soothing sound
As lovers stroll hand in hand all around

I can breathe the air filled with love
Let me stay awhile
To witness the love a little More.

Mother's Love

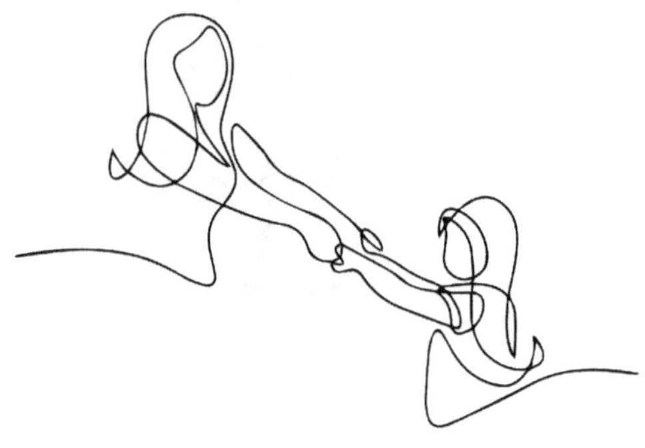

Mother, your love is a true treasure,
You embrace the warmth that never fades
A comfort that chases all fear and shades,

You work all the time, without expecting any
gain
Your love language is different, which has given
me many nicknames

You done everything with love and care,
Which fills our home with warmth and a
protection layer.

I can see my growth in your eyes,
Which lights up and brings new rays (KIRAN)
into my life.

I can witness the suppressed child in you,
Which only comes out when I hold your hand
tight.
That child wants to leave the life again,
Without any fear and with an amazing trail.

You sacrifice all for everyone,
Now it's your time
To live the life you want.

Maa....

Indian Bride

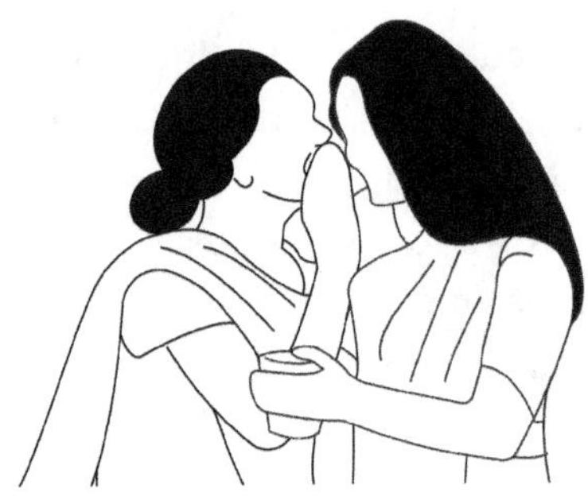

In the land of rising Sun,
Where colour dance and play
A bride adorned in finery, her beauty shines like
jewels.

Her vision of love is holding a tenderness,
Her silken hair flows down her back.

Her eyes are deep like ocean blue,
Which shows life's learning and gratitude,
She is wearing a silk sari,
Her jewels are telling ancient stories while
shining.

Her footsteps are going towards a new life with
the unknown,
She has many things to ask and to say,

But she cannot even see distinctly
Because, she has to be in a veil

She is an Indian bride,
Heart full of purity and,
A complete dedication towards her duty.

Decisions

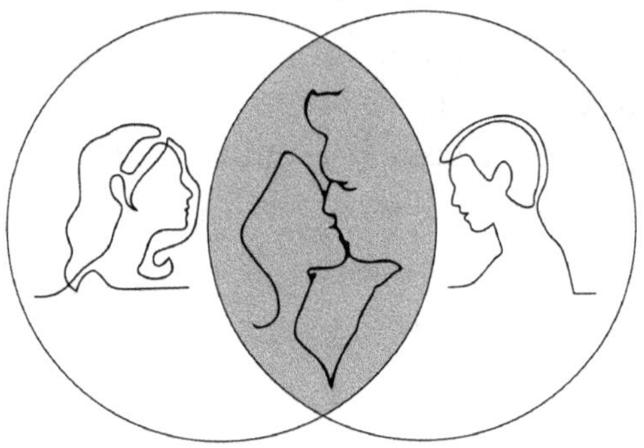

Every decision you make in your life
Has a relation with your past,
Or, the future you design.

Not the same Now

She is not the same,
And she will never be again

Now, she has become an indescribable person,
Woven by many unpleasant events and pain.

She holds all her wounds in the core of her heart,
Like a deep valley in the cascade of mountains.

But, she has chosen to love herself once again
with a storm in her veins.

Teenage

The teenage years, a time to change,
With each step forward, a choice is made,
To embrace the world, or to be dismayed,
To chase dreams, or to hide in fear.

In the teenage period,
Hearts beat with new hope and dreams,
Old one gives advice,
And, familiar age gives the way to new light,
In the realm of adolescence, where hormones
rage.

In the teenage period,
Full of laughter and tears,
A roller coaster ride,
With full of memories and lessons learned,
Which shapes us into who we are today.

Women

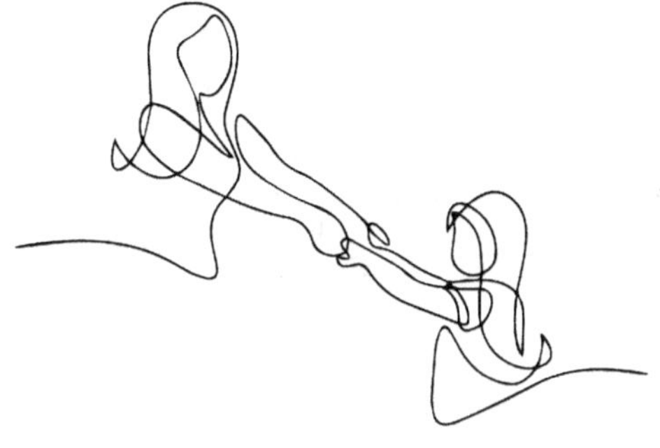

In fields of power, they rise to the top,
Their strength and wisdom never stop.

Their intelligence and wit, a sharp and guiding
light,
Illuminating the path, banishing the night.
Inspiring others to reach for the stars,
With a heart full of love and strength.

A wonder to behold,
A true marvel,
A story to be told.

I want to show you!

I want to show you all the light,
Before any dark patch enters in your life,
Yes! We know
It's normal to face the hard door
It is the cycle of this journey though

I am not the best in every moment,
But I can manage my courage to hold the light
for you,
Maa & Papa
If you need a stick to walk in your old age,
Use our hands forever
If you need help to have your meal
Do not look upon anyone,
Your children are standing with delicious meals
Do not look for any entertainment
As we all together will laugh, love and live
together in our NEST.

SHIVA

A divine of time
A cosmos with secret and shine
A darkness with the source of light
A creator and destructor in a single line
Your 84 roars have given the rhythm to the life
We take birth 84 times and
Ultimately merge in your divine
The universe trembles at your feet
As you meditate on the eternal beat
Your consort goddess Shakti by your side
Together you both embody the cosmic tide.
Praying to you with all my heart
Shambhu, Let me travel under your cover.

School life

In the rooms of learning, where childhood
shaped,
A world of wonder, a world of play,
Where knowledge and joy dance together,
Where the ring of bell was the moment of joy,
Where teachers hold the hand towards learning
scale,
Whether we like anyone or not at that time of
assembly,
We unite in a single lane,
What a wonderful memory of laughter and joy
As I walk through my school gate
I always draw this canvas.

Modern Life

What a morning rush!
A blurred movement and many sound
A symphony of coffee brewing
Phone ringing all around
To make each day count
We grab our gear and fly out the door
With the purpose and passion
We chase our roads
We navigate each day's twists and turns
With hope for a wonderful turn.

Men

Man - You shelter your family
With all your light
You are the real heroes of our daily life
With strength and courage you face all the test
You build the home for our stay
Never demanded much
But given everything without hesitation
Standing strong in every circumstance
A soft heart has faced many challenges.

Hurt

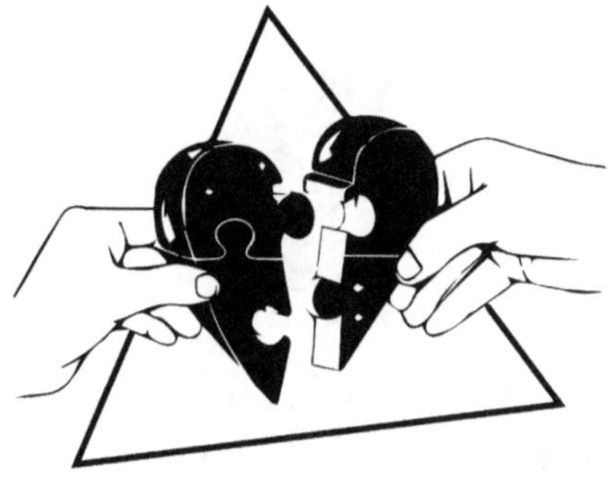

In whispers, I confess my pain
A secret kept in my vein
A burden borne with unspoken words
A scar that's etched in my soul.

Tears of love

With every drop, a memory stays
Of laughter, tears and endless days,
The sorrow's weight, the joy's refrain
Echoes of love that remain the same.

Celebration of Life

The memories we have made
The laughter we have shared
The tears we have cried
The love we have dared
To every moment, every breath
We cherish each one with love and light.

Silence - That Matter

The silence that matters, a sacred space
Where I find my center and my heart's grace
A quiet that nourishes my soul
A peace that makes my spirit whole
Let me embrace the silence a little more
To fill my heart and mind with peace and still
The beauty of silence is a treasure to hold.

9 789363 312869